The You

ing Christie

The Young Christian

Matthew Henry

Christian Focus Publications Ltd.

Published by
Christian Focus Publications Ltd.
Geanies House
Fearn, Tain
Ross-shire IV20 1TW
Scotland
ISBN 0 906731 56 9
This edition © *1987* Christian Focus Publications Ltd.
reprinted 1991
reprinted 1993

Printed and bound in Great Britain by
Cox & Wyman Ltd, Reading

Contents

Introduction

Speak thou the things which become sound doctrine: . . . exhort to be sober minded.
(Titus 2, vv.1,6)

Paul, the aged, is here directing Titus, a young minister, whom he calls his own son in the common faith, what subjects to preach upon; in the choice of which, ministers have need of wisdom — should pray for wisdom — and take direction from this and other scripture-directories.

In general, he must 'speak the things which become sound doctrine,' ver. 1. He must preach the doctrine of Christ — the truth as it is in Jesus — the great mystery of godliness; that is sound, or wholesome doctrine, which is good for food, spiritual food, with which souls are nourished up (*1 Tim. 4, v.6*), and is good for medicine too; it is healing doctrine, as it speaks pardon of sin to those that complain of the terror of guilt, and promises power against sin to those that complain of the strength of corruption; and, blessed be God, this sound, this healing doctrine, is preached to you in its purity, and, I hope, in its power, in season and out of season.

But this is not all, he must speak other things which become this sound doctrine, opposed to those Jewish fables and commandments of men, with which they of the circumcision corrupted the doctrine of Christ (*chap.1, vv.10,14*). The best way to guard against these, will be to preach the duties of Christianity with the doctrines of it — the 'truth which is after godliness.' (*chap. 1, v.1*).

Practical religion, which regulates and governs the heart and life, is that which becomes the doctrine of Christianity — which it becomes the teachers of that doctrine to preach, and both they

7

and the professors of that doctrine to make conscience of. The 'grace of God, that brings salvation, teacheth us' — and therefore the ministers of the word of that grace must teach you — and all that hope for that salvation must learn 'to deny ungodliness, and worldly fleshly lusts, and to live soberly, righteously, and godly.' Right notions will not serve without good morals.

Titus is here particularly directed to preach upon the duties required from Christians of each sex, and each age of life. He must teach aged men how they ought to carry themselves, so as that their 'hoary head,' being found in the way of righteousness, might be 'a crown of glory' to them, ver. 2. And the aged women likewise, ver. 3, that they may teach the young women, ver. 4. And here, in my text, he is directed what application to make to young men.

Thus particular should ministers be in their preaching, that they may, as far as may be, reach everyone's case, which is the likeliest way to reach everyone's conscience. Thus ministers must endeavour rightly to divide the word of truth, and as wise and faithful stewards in God's house, to give every one their portion of meat in due season. And O that every one would take their portion, and feed upon it, and digest it; and instead of saying, 'This was for such a one,' would learn to say, 'This is for me!'.

In dealing with young men, he is here directed to exhort them. He must instruct them what to do, that they might know their duty; he must put them in mind of it, that they might know it, then when they had occasion to do it; he must excite and stir them up to it, and urge it upon them with motives and arguments; and he must encourage them in the doing of it, and comfort them that they might go on in it cheerfully. All this is included in the word here used for exhorting them; and there is need for all this, and all is little enough; for some are ignorant, and need to be taught — others are careless, and need to be quickened; some think their duty an indifferent thing, and on such we must press the command which makes it necessary — others think it an impracticable thing, and to such we must preach the grace that makes it easy.

In pressing practical godliness, it is hard to say which is more merciful — persuasion or direction; and which will be more serviceable to our end — good rules, to show us what we should do — or good reasons, to convince us that it is our duty and interest to do it. Perhaps some stand in more need of the one, some of the other; and the scripture furnishes us with abundant matter for both, enough to furnish the man of God for every good word of this kind.

The original word might properly be rendered, to *call to* or *call upon*, and this is the work of ministers to be your monitors. We call to you, we call upon you, frequently, and with importunity, and as we see occasion, to mind your duty and not to trifle in it, to take heed of sin and not expose yourselves to it. This is the word behind you, which is promised (*Isa. 30, v.21*), which shall say, 'This is the way, walk ye in it, when ye turn to the right hand and when ye turn to the left.'

Titus must exhort them in his public preaching, and in that must choose out words to reason with them. The rulers of the Jewish synagogue, after the reading of the laws and prophets in the assembly, on the Sabbath, desired of Paul a 'word of exhortation for the people' (*Acts 13, v.15*), and public exhortations to those of one age, relation, or condition, may be of use to others, who are not to sit by as unconcerned, but some way or other to accommodate it to themselves, for what we say unto some, we say unto all.

Yet this was not enough, he must exhort them in his personal converse, with them — must visit them at their houses, and there give them this admonition — must give it in particular manner to those that he saw needed it — give it with application — in this and the other instance, you must be of a better spirit, and carry it better. When he was in company with young men, he must be giving them good advice, and instead of allowing himself to be vain as they were, endeavour to make them grave as he was.

Ministers must preach not only in the pulpit, but out of it; their converse must be a constant sermon, and in that they may be more particular in the application, and descend to persons and cases better than they can in their public ministry. Those ministers who complain they would do this statedly and solemnly, but cannot bring it to bear, can yet have no excuse for not doing it occasionally when it comes in their way, nor would seek an excuse if they had but a heart to it.

That which he must exhort them to, is to be sober-minded. All the law that concerns them in particular, is summed up in this one word, exhort them to be sober-minded. It is a very significant, comprehensive word; and has in it a check to all the ill habits and ill courses that are so mischievous and ruining to young people. The word speaks the duty of young men, but it is likewise twice used in the directory for young women, ver. 4, 'That they may teach the young women to be sober,' that they may sober the young women, may give them such instructions and examples as may help to make them sober; and again, ver. 5, that they may teach them to be discreet; so that it is the duty of young women, as well as young men, to be sober-minded. It is an exhortation proper for both the sexes of that age; and it is my exhortation to all of that age, that are within hearing to-day; I 'beseech you suffer this word of exhortation;' reject it at your peril, for if it comes from God, it is your utmost peril to refuse it.

PART ONE

What is a Sober Mind?

Let us see what it is that we press upon you when we exhort you to be sober-minded. And I shall keep to the original word used in my text, and the various meanings of it. It is the same word that is used to set forth the third part of our Christian duty, and is put first of the three lessons which the grace of God teacheth us, to live soberly, ver. 12. And in another place, it is put last of three excellent Christian graces: God hath given us 'the spirit of power, and of love, and of a sound mind' (*2 Tim. 1, v.7*).

1. Considerate
2. Cautious
3. Humble
4. Self-denying
5. Gentle
6. Chaste
7. Composed
8. Content
9. Serious

1. Considerate

You must be considerate and thoughtful, and not rash and
heedless. To be sober-minded, is to make use of our reason, in
reasoning with ourselves and in communing with our own
hearts — to employ those noble powers and capacities, by which
we are distingushed from, and dignified above the beasts, for
those great ends for which we were endued with them, that we
may not receive the grace of God in them in vain, but being
rational creatures, may act rationally, as behoves us, as becomes
us. You learned to talk when you were children, when will you
learn to think — to think seriously — to think to the purpose?
Floating thoughts your heads are full of, foreign and impertinent ones, when will you be brought to close and fixed thoughts,
to think with concern and application of the great things that
belong to your everlasting peace and welfare?

Some have recommended the study of the mathematics, as
proper to fix the minds of young people, and bring them to
think. I wish any thing would do it, but would much rather it
were done by a deep concern about the soul and another world,
which, if it once prevail, will effectively fix the thoughts, and to
the best purpose; for when once you come to see the greatness of
that God with whom you have to do, and the weight of that
eternity you are standing upon the brink of, you will see it is
time to think, high time to look about you.

Learn to think not only of what is just before you, which
strikes the senses, and affects the imagination, but of the causes
and consequences, and reasons of things; to discover truths, to
compare them with one another, to argue upon them and apply
them to yourselves, and to bring them to a head; not to fasten
upon that which doth come first into your minds, but upon that
which should come first, and which deserves to be first considered.

Multitudes are undone because they are unthinking; inconsideration is the ruin of thousands, and many a precious soul
perisheth through mere carelessness. 'Now therefore, thus saith
the Lord of hosts, consider your ways;' retire into your own
souls, begin an acquaintance with them; it will be the most

profitable acquaintance you can fall into, and will turn to the
best account. While you are coveting to see the world, and to be
acquainted with it, be not strangers at home.

Take time to think, desire to be alone now and then, and let
not solitude and retirement be an uneasiness to you, for you
have a heart of your own that you may find talk with, and a God
nigh unto you, with whom you may have a pleasing communion.

Learn to think freely; God invites you to do so: 'Come now,
and let us reason together.' We desire not you should take things
upon trust, but inquire impartially into them, as the noble
Bereans, who searched the scriptures daily, whether those
things were so which the apostles told them. Pure Christianity
and serious godliness fear not the scrutiny of a free thought, but
despise the impotent malice of a prejudiced one.

There are those, I find, who, under the pretence of being
free-thinkers, by sly insinuations endeavour to shock young
people's belief of the divine authority of the scriptures, and
undermine all revealed religion, by turning sacred things into
jest and ridicule; but they usurp the honourable character of
free-thinkers — it does not belong to them — they are as far
from the freedom they pretend to, as they are from the sincerity
they protest against; for it is certain, pride and affectation of
singularity, and a spirit of opposition and contradiction, do as
much enslave the thoughts on the one hand, as an implicit faith
and obedience on the other hand. While they promise men
liberty, they do but deceive them; and, under colour of being
sole masters of reason, and ridiculing all that agree not with
them, they as arbitrarily impose upon men's credulity, as ever
popes and councils did under colour of being sole masters of
faith and anathematizing all that differ from them.

Learn to think for yourselves — to think of yourselves — to
think with application. Think what you are, and what you are
capable of; think who made you, and what you were made for;
for what end you were endowed with the powers of reason, and
attended by the inferior creatures; think what you have been
doing since you came into the world — of the great work you

were sent into the world about — of the vanity of childhood and youth — and how unavoidably the years of them are past away as a tale that is told — and whether therefore it be not time, high time, for the youngest of you to begin to be religious and to enter in at the strait gate.

And as to your particular actions, do not walk at all adventures, as those do that despise their own ways, but consider what you do before you do it, that you may not have occasion to repent of it afterwards; do nothing rashly, but always speak and act under the government of the great law of consideration. Ponder the path of your feet, that it may be a straight path.

Some people take a pride in being careless; tell them of such and such a thing that they were warned about, they turn it off with this excuse, that for their parts they never heed, they mind not what is said to them; nor ever thought of it since; and so they glory in their shame. But be not you thus negligent; for then, and not till then, there begins to be hopes to set their hearts to all those things that are testified unto them, and to think of them with the reason of men, and the concern they deserve.

2. Cautious

You must be cautious, and prudent, and not wilful and heady. The word in the text is the same that is rendered, ver. 5, to be *discreet*. You must not only think rationally, but when you have done so, you must act wisely, and so as will be most for your true interest; walk circumspectly, look before you, look about you, look under your feet, and pick your way, not as fools, but as wise.

David's purpose when he set out in the world, was, 'I will behave myself wisely in a perfect way;' and his prayer was, 'Lord, when wilt thou come unto me?' (*Ps. 101, v.2*). And accordingly we find (*1 Sam. 18, v.14*) his purpose performed, and his prayer answered, 'He behaved himself wisely in all his ways, and the Lord was with him.' Those that govern themselves, God will guide, but will justly leave those that love to wander, to wander endlessly.

Put away childish follies with other childish things, and do not all your days think and speak as children. Espouse principles of wisdom; fix to yourselves rules of wisdom, and be ruled by those rules, and acted by those principles. It is the wisdom of the prudent to understand his own way, his own business, not to censure other people's; and this wisdom will in all cases be profitable to direct what measures, what steps, to take.

Youth is apt to be bold and venturous, and therefore resolute and peremptory, to its great prejudice. But be not you so; let reason and conscience, according to the duty of their place, give check to the violence of appetite and passion; let them rectify the mistakes, and over-rule the hasty dictates of humour and fancy, and reduce the arbitrary and exorbitant power of those tyrants.

How often does Solomon press it upon the young man he takes under his tuition? 'My son, be wise; wisdom is the principal thing, therefore get wisdom, get understanding.' You that are launching out into the world must take wisdom to be your pilot, or you are in danger of splitting upon some rock or other; this must be your pillar of cloud and fire, which you must follow the conduct of through this wilderness.

Be diffident of your own judgments, and jealous of yourselves, that you do not take things right, or not take them entire, and for that reason afraid lest the resolutions, which are the result of your considerations, should prove wrong, and therefore leave room for second thoughts. Say not, 'I *will* do so and so — I am resolved I will, whatever may be said to the contrary. I will walk in the way of my heart, and in the sight of my eyes, whatever it cost me.' Never have any will but what is guided by wisdom.

Therefore in every case of moment and difficulty, be willing to be advised by your friends, and depend more upon their judgment who have had longer experience of the world, than upon your own. Consult with those that are wise and good; ask them what they would do if they were in your case, and you will find, that 'in the multitude of counsellors there is safety;' and that often times proves best which was least your own doing; or if it should not prove well, it will be a satisfaction to you, that you did not do it without advice and mature deliberation, and that as the thing appeared then, you did it for the best.

What brighter character can be given of a young man, than to say, he is wise? or what blacker, than to say, he is wilful? See the former in Solomon, who calls himself a child, 'I know not how to go out, or to come in' (*1 Kings 3, v.7*); and yet his father calls him a wise man, that knows what he is to do. See the latter in the character of the rebellious son, that was to be stoned to death, against whom the indictment runs thus, 'He is stubborn, he will not obey the voice of his father and mother' (*Deut. 21, vv.18,20*). Those are the fools whom there is little hope of, that despise wisdom and instruction (*Prov. 1, v.7*). He that will not be counselled, cannot be helped.

But would you be wise — not only to be thought so, but really be so? Study the scriptures; by them you will get more understanding than the ancients, than all your teachers (*Ps. 119, vv.99,100*). Make your observations upon the carriage and miscarriage of others, that you may take a pattern by those that do well, and take warning by those that do ill, may look upon both, and receive instruction. But especially be earnest with God in prayer for wisdom, as Solomon was; and the prayer was both pleasing and prevailing in heaven. 'If any man,' if any young man 'lack wisdom,' and is sensible that he lacks it, he is directed what to do, his way is plain, 'let him ask of God;' and, he is encouraged to do it; 'for the Lord giveth wisdom.' He has it to give (*Prov. 2, v.6*). He delights to give it; he gives liberally; he has a particular eye to young people in the dispensing of this gift, for his word was written 'to give to the young man knowledge and discretion' (*Prov. 1, v.4*).

And because some are willing to be counselled, but do not care to be rebuked, we are told that he gives, and upbraids not; yet as if this were not encouragement enough to beggars at Wisdom's gates, there is an express promise to every one that seeks aright, that he shall not seek in vain; it is not a promise with a perhaps, but with the greatest assurance, 'it shall be given him' (*James 1, v.5*). To all true believers, Christ himself is, and shall be made of God, wisdom (*1 Cor. 1, v.30*).

3. Humble

You must be humble and modest, 'and not proud and conceited.' It is recommended to the younger to be clothed with humility (*1 Pet. 5, v.5*), that is, to be sober-minded.

It is an observation I have made upon that little acquaintance I have had with the world, that I have seen more young people ruined by pride, than perhaps by any one lust whatsoever; and therefore let me press this upon you with all earnestness; and it is a caution introduced with more than ordinary solemnity (*Rom. 12, v.3*). 'I say, through the grace given unto me, unto every man that is among you;' and what is the word that is thus declared to be of divine original, and universal concern? it is this; that 'no man think of himself more highly than he ought to think, but think soberly.'

Keep up low thoughts of yourselves — of your endowments both outward and inward; of your attainments and improvements, and all your performances, and all the things you call merits and excellencies. Boast not of a false gift — of what you have not; nor be puffed up with what you have. What there is in you that is commendable, wink at it yourselves, as most people do at their own faults, and diminish it, and look much at that in others which is more commendable. Let not the handsome glory in their beauty, nor the ingenious in their wit, for there cannot be a greater allay to the glory than to have it said, such and such are comely, and witty, but they know it. Doth your face in any respect shine? be as Moses was, he wist not that the skin of his face shone; and do what Moses did, as soon as he perceived it, he put a vail upon it. Delight more to say and do what is praiseworthy, than to be praised for it; for 'what hast thou which thou hast not received?' and what hast thou received which thou has not abused? and why then dost thou boast?

Keep up a quick and constant sense of your own manifold defects and infirmities; how much there is in you, and how much is said and done by you every day, which you have reason to be ashamed of, and humbled for; in how many things you come short of others, and in how many more you come short of the rule; you will find no reason to be proud of what you know,

17

when you see how much you are ignorant of, nor of what you do that is good, when you see how much you do amiss. Dwell much upon humbling considerations, and those that tend to take down your high opinion of yourselves; and keep up a humble sense of your necessary and constant dependence upon Christ and his grace, without which you are nothing, and will soon be worse than nothing.

Think not yourselves too wise, too good, too old to be reproved for what is amiss, and to be taught to do better. When you are double and treble the age you are, yet you will not be too old to learn, and increase in learning. 'If any man thinks that he knows any thing,' that he knows every thing, so as that he needs no more instruction, 'he knoweth nothing yet as he ought to know it' (*1 Cor. 8, v.2*). And therefore he that seems to be wise — seems so to himself — seems so to others — 'let him become a fool, that he may be wise;' let him be sensible of his own folly, that he may be quickened to use the means of wisdom, and prepared to receive the grace of wisdom, (*1 Cor. 3, v.18*).

Be not confident of your own judgment, nor opinionative, nor look upon those with contempt that do not think as you do. Elihu is a great example of humility and modesty to those of your age; he was swift to hear, and very ambitious to learn, for it is the learning age: 'I am young, and you are old, and therefore I waited for your words, I gave ear to your reasons, I attended unto you' — ready to give what you said its due weight, and expecting to hear something that I had not known before; but he was slow to speak, 'I was afraid, and durst not show you my opinion,' for 'I said, Days should speak' (*Job 32, vv.6,7,11,12*). Be not forward to say, 'I hold so and so,' for — as a grave divine once told a novice that was laying down the law with great assurance — 'It best becomes you to hold your peace.'

Take heed of thinking yourselves above your business. You that are apprentices, think not yourself above your service: humility will make the yoke you are under easy to you, which will gall the proud and stiff neck. You that are set up for yourselves, think it no disparagement to you to confine yourselves to your business, and to make a business of it — to see to it with your own eyes, no, nor to put your own hands to it. Be ashamed of nothing but sin.

It will be yet much worse, if you think yourselves above your religion — above the restraints of it, as if it were a thing below you to be afraid of sin, and to make conscience of your words and actions, whereas there cannot be a greater disgrace to you, than loose walking. Nor above the exercise of religion, as if it were a thing below you to pray, and hear the word, and join in acts of devotion, for it is really the greatest honour you can do yourselves thus to honour God.

Let this branch of sober-mindedness appear in your looks and carriage; let the show of your countenance witness for you, that you are not confident and conceited, but that you keep up a due diffidence of yourselves, and a due deference to all about you, especially those above you. Be not pert in your carriage, nor outrageous in your dress.

If there be any thing in the garb and carriage that young people may be innocently proud of, because those about them will be justly pleased with it, it is the gravity of it, when it is an indication of humility and modesty reigning in the heart; for those are the best ornaments, and, in the sight of God, and all wise men, of great price; and you will find, that 'better it is to be of a humble spirit with the lowly, than to divide the spoil with the proud;' for when 'men's pride shall bring them low, honour shall uphold the humble in spirit,' and they shall be upheld, borne up, and borne out, in that honour.

4. Self-denying

You must be temperate and self-denying, and not indulgent of your appetites. It is the same word in the text, that in ver. 2 is translated temperate, and is one of the lessons that the aged men must learn; and some think it properly signifies a moderate use of meat and drink, so as to keep the mean, and, in the use of them, to save our mind from being clouded, and our wisdom from being corrupted, that is, our hearts from being over-charged with surfeiting and drunkenness. We commonly put a sober man in opposition to one that is drunk, or addicted to drunkenness.

Let me therefore warn young men to dread the sin of drunkenness; keep at a distance from it; avoid all appearances of it, and approaches towards it. It has slain its thousands — its ten thousands of young people; has ruined their health, brought diseases upon them, and cut them off in the flower of their days. How many fall unpitied sacrifices to this base lust! It has ruined their estates and trades at their first setting out; when the time that should have been spent in the shop and warehouse, is spent in the tavern and alehouse — when the money they should buy goods with, and pay their debts with, is thrown away in the gratification of an inordinate love of wine and strong drink — no wonder if they soon break, and flee their country.

Take heed of the beginnings of this sin, for the way of it is downhill; and many, under pretence of an innocent entertainment, and passing the evening in a pleasant conversation, are drawn in to drink to excess, and make beasts of themselves; and you should tremble to think how fatal the consequences of it are — how unfit it renders you for the service of God at night, yea, and for your own business the next morning — how many are thus besotted, and sunk into that drowsiness which clothes a man with rags; and yet that is not the worst — it extinguishes convictions and sparks of devotion — and provokes the Spirit of grace to withdraw — and it will be the sinner's eternal ruin, if it be not repented of, and forsaken in time; for it shall not be unsaid, it cannot be gainsaid, that 'drunkards shall not inherit the kingdom of God.'

'Look not then upon the wine when it is red, when it gives its colour in the cup,' is charming, is tempting; be not overcome by its allurements, for at the last it 'bites like a serpent, and stings like an adder.' If you saw the devil putting the cup of drunkenness into your hand, I dare say, you would not take it out of his: you may be sure the temptation to it comes from him, and therefore ought to dread it as much as if you saw it. If you saw poison put into the glass, you would not drink it; and if it be provoking to God, and ruining to your souls, it is worse than poison; there is worse than death, there is hell in the cup, and will you not then refuse it? How many ways may you spend your evening, when you are fatigued with the business of the day, better than in drinking, in immoderate drinking?

I am sorry we cannot urge against you, so much as gladly we would, the scandal of it — it is grown so fashionable. But whether you will hear, or whether you will forbear, we will insist upon the sin of it, and its prejudice to the soul both here and for ever, and beg of you in consideration of this, to frighten yourselves from it; we will insist likewise upon the real disgrace that it is to a reasonable creature, who is hereby spoiled of his crown, and levelled with the brutes, and beg of you in consideration of this, to shame yourselves out of it before God and your own conscience.

It is a sin that is in a special manner shameful and hurtful to those who profess religion. You that have been well-educated, that have been bred up in sober families, have had examples of sobriety set you, and have known that the honours and pleasures of a sober conversation are, if, when you set up for yourselves, you think yourselves happy in getting clear from the restraints of a sober regimen, and take the liberty of the drunkards, what a reproach will it be to you! what a degeneracy! what a fall from your first love! and where will it stop? Perhaps you have given up your names to the Lord Jesus at his table, and dare you partake of the cup of the Lord, and the cup of devils?

Let Christians that are made to our God kings and priests, take to themselves the lesson which Solomon's mother taught him, 'It is not for kings, O Lemuel, it is not for kings;' so it is not for Christians, 'to drink wine,' but with great moderation, 'lest they drink and forget the law,' forget the gospel (*Prov. 31, vv.4,5*).

Yet this is not all I have to warn you against under this head; let not young people be nice and curious in their diet, nor solicitous to have all the delights of sense wound up to the height of pleasurableness; be 'not desirous of dainties, for they are deceitful meat' (*Prov. 23, v.3*). It is true, the use of them is lawful, but it is as true that the love of them is dangerous; and

21

the indulging of the appetites of the body to them is oft prejudicial to the soul and its true interests.

Learn betimes to relish the delights that are rational and spiritual, and then your mouths will be out of taste to those pleasures that are brutal, and belong only to the animal life; and be afraid lest by indulging the body and the lusts of it, you come by degrees to the black character of those that were 'lovers of pleasure, more than lovers of God' (*2 Tim. 3, v.4*).

The body is made to be a servant to the soul, and it must be treated accordingly; we must give it, as we must to our servants, that which is just and equal; let it have what is fitting, but let it not be suffered to domineer, for nothing is so insufferable as 'a servant when he reigneth' (*Prov. 30, v.22*); nor let it be pampered, for 'he that delicately brings up his servant from a child, shall have him become his son at the length' (*Prov. 29, v.21*).

Be dead therefore to the delights of sense; mortify the love of ease and pleasure — learn betimes to endure hardness — use yourselves to deny yourselves — and so you will make it easy to yourselves, and will the better bear the common calamities of human life, as well as sufferings for righteousness-sake. Those that would approve themselves good soldiers of Jesus Christ, must endure hardness, must inure themselves to it (*2 Tim. 2, v.3*).

5. Gentle

You must be mild and gentle, and not indulgent of your passions. The word here used signifies moderation, such a soundness of mind as is opposed to frenzy and violence. We have need of sobriety to restrain and repress not only our inordinate appetites towards those things that are pleasing to sense, but our irregular resentment of those things that are displeasing; for such a vexatious knowledge of good and evil has mankind got by eating of the forbidden tree.

Young people are especially apt to be hot and furious, to resent injuries, and to study revenge, like Simeon and Levi, whose anger was cursed, for it was fierce; and their wrath, for it was cruel; and therefore the passion is ungoverned, because the pride is unmortified. They are fond of liberty, and therefore cannot bear control; and wedded to their own opinion, and therefore cannot bear contradiction, but are all in a flame presently, if any one cross them; and they reckon that an honour, which is really their shame — to lay the reins on the neck of their passions, not caring what indecencies they are transported into by them, nor considering how mischievous the consequences may be.

Learn betimes to bridle your anger — to guard against the sparks of provocation, that they may not fall into the tinder; or, if the fire be kindled, put it out presently, by commanding the peace in your own souls, and setting a watch before the door of your lips. And when at any time you are affronted, or think yourselves so, aim not at the wit of a sharp answer, which will stir up anger, but at the wisdom and grace of a soft answer, which will turn away wrath (*Prov. 15, v.1*).

You are setting out in the world, and would have your passage through it comfortable. Now there is nothing will contribute more to that than a quiet spirit: 'The meek shall inherit the earth,' was God's promise, by David first (*Ps. 37, v.11*); and afterwards by the Son of David (*Mat. 5, v.5*); and that if they possess not an abundance of wealth, yet they shall delight themselves in the abundance of peace. By the good government of your passions, you will make yourselves easy, and easy to those about you; and a great deal of mischief both to others and to yourselves will be prevented.

The moral philosophers valued themselves very much upon the power which their instructions had upon young people, to soften and sweeten their temper, and teach them to govern their passions, and keep a strict hand upon them. And shall Christianity, which, to all the arguments which reason suggests for meekness, adds the authority of the God that made us, forbidding rash anger, as heart-murder — the example of the Lord Jesus Christ that bought us, and bids us learn of him to be meek and lowly in heart — the consolations of the Spirit, which have a direct tendency to make us pleasant to ourselves and others — and our experiences of God's mercy and grace in forbearing and forgiving us — shall this divine and heavenly institution come short of their instructions, in plucking up this root of bitterness which bears gall and wormwood, and making us peaceful, gentle, and easy to be entreated, which are the bright and blessed characters of the wisdom from above? (*James 3, v.17*).

If you suffer your passions to get head now you are young, they will be in danger of growing more and more headstrong, and of making you perpetually uneasy; but if you get dominion over them now, you will easily keep dominion, and so keep the peace in your hearts and houses, and through the grace of God, it will not be in the power even of sickness or old age to make you peevish, to sour your temper, or embitter your spirits. Put on therefore among the ornaments of your youth, 'as the elect of God, holy and beloved, bowels of mercies, kindness, humbleness of mind, meekness and long-suffering.' Your age is made for love; let holy love therefore be a law to you.

6. Chaste

You must be chaste and reserved, and not wanton and impure. When it is here made the particular duty of young men, this meaning of the word must certainly be taken in, for the 'lusts of the flesh which are manifest, adultery, fornication, uncleanness, and lasciviousness' (*Gal. 5. v.19*), are particularly called youthful lusts.

Against those, in Christ's name, I am here to warn all you that are young. For God's sake, and for your own precious soul's sake, flee these youthful lusts; dread them as you would a devouring fire, or a destroying plague, and keep at a distance from them; 'Abstain from all appearances of these sins: hating even the garment spotted with the flesh,' even the attire of an harlot. Covet not to know these depths of Satan, but take a pride in being ignorant of the way of the adulterous woman. See all temptations to uncleanness coming from the unclean spirit, that roaring lion who goes about continually, thus seeking to devour young people.

O that you would betimes conceive a detestation and abhorrence of this sin, as much below you, and more against you; and put on a firm and steady resolution in the strength of the grace of Jesus Christ, never to defile yourselves with it; remembering what the apostle prescribes, as that which ought to be the constant care of the unmarried, to be holy both in body and spirit, and so to please the Lord (*1 Cor. 7, v.34*).

Take heed of the beginnings of this sin, lest Satan in any thing get advantage against you, and the little thief, stolen in insensibly at the window, open the door to the great one. How earnestly doth Solomon warn his young man to take heed of the baits, lest he be taken in the snares of the evil woman! 'Remove thy way far from her,' saith he, for he that would be kept from harm, must keep out of harm's way; 'come not nigh the door of her house,' but go on the other side of the street, as thou wouldst, if it were a house infected; lest thou mourn at the last, when thy flesh and thy body are consumed, and say, 'How have I hated instruction, and my heart despised reproof?' (*Prov. 5, vv.8,11,12*).

Pray earnestly to God for his grace to keep you from this sin, and that it may be sufficient for you; so as that, be the temptation never so sudden, it may find you awake, and aware of it, that you may not be surprised into it: and be it never so strong, it may find you armed against it, with the whole armour of God, that you may not be overpowered, and overcome by it.

Get your hearts purified by the word of God, and sanctified by divine love, for how else shall young people cleanse their way, but by taking heed thereto, according to the word? Keep up the authority of conscience, and keep it always tender, and void of offence. Make a covenant with your eyes, that they may not be the inlets of any impure desires; and pray David's prayer, 'Turn away mine eyes from beholding vanity;' that you may never look and lust.

Modesty is the hedge of chastity, and it is the ornament of your age, therefore be sure to keep that up. Let your dress and carriage be very modest, and such as speaks a chaste conversation coupled with fear. Make it to appear that you know how to be pleasant and cheerful without transgressing even the strictest rules of modesty; nay, that you know not how to be so, when any thing is said or done against those rules.

I would especially charge you that are young, to take heed that no corrupt filthy communication proceed out of your mouth. Never dare to speak, nor delight to hear any thing that is immodest; 'fornication, and all uncleanness, let it not be once named among you:' it is foolish talking and jesting 'which is not convenient,' which is very unbecoming the professors of such a pure and undefiled religion as Christianity is; it is that 'evil communication' which corrupts good manners; it is, as some think, that 'idle word' for which our Saviour saith we must give account in the great day.

Think what a great dishonour lascivious talk is to God — what a reproach to yourselves — and what mischief it doth to those you converse with; how great a matter a spark of this fire from hell may kindle; and how much of the sin and ruin of souls you may hereby have to answer for. God turns those to a pure language whom he brings to call upon his name (*Zeph. 3, v.9*).

7. Composed

You must be staid and composed, and not giddy and unsettled. This we commonly take to be signified by a sober mind — a mind that acts and moves steadily, and is one with itself; in opposition to a roving wandering heart, a heart divided, which cannot but be found faulty. Be sober-minded, that is, let your hearts be fixed (*Ps. 108, v.1*). Stablish your hearts, and be not like Reuben 'unstable as water,' for those that are so will never excel. Fix now, in the days of your youth, for God and Christ, and serious godliness; fix for heaven as your end, and holiness as your way. Halt no longer, hover no longer between two, but be at a point; you have often been bid to choose whom you will serve, stand no longer deliberating, but bring this matter at length to the issue you will abide by, and abide by it, 'Nay, but we will serve the Lord.'

Fix to that, whatever it is, that you are designed for in the world; fix to your business — fix to your book, if that is to be.

Whatever it is that you are employed in, let your application to it be close and constant, and do not upon every slight and trivial pretence start aside from it, and say you are weary of it, or you hope to mend yourselves, when the same volatile humour that makes you uneasy in the place and work you are in, will soon make you so in another.

Learn to fix your thoughts, and be not wandering; let them not run from one thing to another, as the bird in wandering, and the swallow in flying, for thus they run at length with the fool's eyes unto the ends of the earth; but what your hand finds to do, and your heart to think of, which is to the purpose, do it and think it with all your might, and pursue it close, till you bring it to an issue, and then it is done and thought to purpose indeed; what you do, mind your business.

Learn to fix your aims, and act with a single eye; for the double-minded man, who is far from being sober-minded, cannot but be unstable in all his ways, and turns himself as the wind turns, and 'he that wavereth is like a wave of the sea' (*James 1, vv.6,8*). Act considerately, that is, consistently with yourselves: and as those that understand your own ways, and have not your ear open to every whisper and suggestion that would turn you out of it. Be no more children tossed to and fro with every wind, enticed to and fro with every bait (*Eph. 4, v.14*), but in understanding be ye men, be ye fixed; let your foot stand in an even place, and then let your hearts be established — be not moved — be not removed.

8. Content

You must be content and easy, and not ambitious and aspiring. Some make the word to signify the bringing of the mind down to the condition, when the condition will not in every thing be brought up to the mind. A sober mind is that which accommodates itself to every estate of life, and every event of providence, so that whatever changes happen, it preserves the possession and enjoyment of itself.

You that are young, must learn betimes to reconcile yourselves to your lot, and make the best of that which is, because it is the will of God it should be as it is, and what pleases him ought to please us; for he knows what is fit to be done, and fit for us to have, better than we do. Let this check all disquieting discontented thoughts.

Should it be according to your mind? Shall you who are but of yesterday control him, quarrel with him, or prescribe to him, whose counsels were of old from everlasting? It is folly to direct the divine disposals, but wisdom to acquiesce in them. He who determineth the times before appointed, and the bounds of men's habitation, ordered what our rank and station should be in the world — what parents we should be born of — what lot we should be born to — and what our make and capacity of mind and body should be.

And in these respects there is a great variety ordained by providence between some and others, who yet are made of one blood; some are born to wealth and honour, others to poverty and obscurity; some seem made and marked by Nature, that is, the God of nature, to be great and considerable, while others seem doomed to be all their days little, and low.

You see many above you, that make a figure in the world, and are likely to do so yet more, while you are but as cyphers, yet do not envy them, nor fret at the place God's providence has put you in, but make yourselves easy in it, and make the best of it, as those who are satisfied not only in general, that all is well that God doth, but in particular, all is well that he doth with you.

Possess your minds, now you are young, with a reverence for the divine providence, its sovereignty, wisdom, and goodness; and bring your minds unto a cheerful reference of yourselves to all its arbitrations; 'Here I am, let the Lord do with me, and all mine affairs, as seemeth good in his sight.' This would have a mighty influence upon the conduct of your affairs, and the evenness of your spirits, all your days.

Whatever you are dispossessed of, or disturbed in the enjoyment of, resolve to be easy — not because you cannot help it; this is an evil, and I must bear it; that is but a poor reason — but because it is the will of God, whose will is his wisdom; this is an evil, but it is designed for my good, and I will bear it.

Lay your expectations low from this world, and promise not yourselves great matters in it. It is God's command (*Rom 12, v.16*), 'Mind not high things,' set not your eyes and hearts upon them, as if they were the best things, and as if they would make you happy, and you could not be happy without them; 'but condescend to men of low estate,' and take as much pleasure in converse with them, as if they were company for princes and peers; or, as the margin reads it, 'Be content with mean things' — with a mean habitation, mean diet, mean clothes, mean employments, if such be your lot — and instead of blaming it, bless God for it, that it is not worse, and believe it is fittest for you.

Not that I would have young people mean-spirited, or cramped in their aims and endeavours. Whatever your business is, strive to be excellent and eminent in it; whatever your substance is, be diligent, that, by the blessing of God upon it, it may, like Job's, be increased in the land. A good man leaves an inheritance, honestly got, to his children's children. But I would not have you ambitious of great things; covet not by taking thought to add cubits to your stature. Let it suffice to thrive by inches, with the increases of the sober-minded, that do not make haste to be rich; for soft and fair goes far.

We commonly say of you that are young, that you are upon your preferment; shall I persuade you to reckon it your best preferment to be eminently pious, and serviceable to the glory of God, and the interests of his kingdom in the world; that is the way to have the best reputation among men, which wise men reckon no despicable preferment, for 'a good name is better than precious ointment.' Aim at advancing yourselves, not that you may live in so much the more pomp and ease, but that you may be in so much the better capacity to do good, and that is true preferment.

We commonly say of you that are young, that now is your time to make your fortune. It is a heathenish expression, for it is not blind fortune, but an all-seeing providence that we are governed by. But that is not all; it is not in your power to make your own lot; 'every man's judgment proceedeth from the

Lord;' every creature is that to you, and no more than he makes it to be; and therefore you must seek his favour; and reckon your lot best made, when you have 'the Lord to be the portion of your inheritance and your cup;' and then say, 'The lines are fallen to you in pleasant places.' That is best for you, which is best for your souls, and in that you must soberly rest satisfied.

Jacob was setting out in the world, and going to take him a wife, when all he desired and aimed at, and, if I may so say, indented for in his marriage-articles, was bread to eat, and raiment to put on, to be kept in his way, and brought at length to his father's house in peace; and why should any of the spiritual seed of Jacob look higher in this world, who knows and hopes he has eternal riches in reversion after one life? Let young people be modest and moderate, and sober-minded in their desires and expectations of temporal good things, as becomes those who see through them, and look above and beyond them, to the things not seen, that are eternal.

9. Serious

You must be grave and serious, and not frothy and vain. This meaning we commonly give to the word here used. Him that is serious, we call a sober man; and I put this last of the ingredients of this sober-mindedness, because it will have a very great influence upon all the rest; we should gain our point entirely with young people, if we could but prevail with them to be serious. It is serious piety we would bring them to, and to live in good earnest.

Not that we would oblige young people never to be merry, or had any ill-natured design upon them to make them melancholy; no, religion allows them to be cheerful; it is your time, make your best of it: evil days will come, of which you will say you have no pleasure in them, when the cares and sorrows of this world increase upon you, and we would not have you to anticipate those evil days. It is mentioned as an instance of the promised prosperity and flourishing state of Jerusalem, that the streets of the city shall be full of boys, and girls playing in the streets thereof (*Zech. 8, v.5*).

Nay, religion prescribes cheerfulness to all those that are sincere and hearty in it: 'Go thy way, eat thy bread with joy, and drink thy wine with a merry heart, for God now accepteth thy works' (*Eccl. 9, v.7*), God expects to be served by us with 'joyfulness and with gladness of heart, for the abundance of all things' (*Deut. 28, v.47*). And it is certain, that none have such good reason to be cheerful as godly people have; none can be so upon better grounds, or with a better grace; so justly, or so safely. I have often said — and I must take all occasions to repeat it — that a holy heavenly life, spent in the service of God, and in communion with him, is without doubt the most pleasant, comfortable life any one can live in this world.

But that which I would caution you against under this head, is vain and carnal mirth — that mirth — that laughter of the fool — of which Solomon says, 'it is mad, and what doth it?' Innocent mirth is of good use in its time and place; it will revive the spirit, and fit you for business; 'a merry heart doth good like a medicine;' but then it must be used like a medicine — must be taken physically; only when there is occasion for it, and not constantly like our daily bread; and, like medicine, it must be then not too often, so not too much at a time, like opiates, which are taken by drops, and with great caution. When you make use of these medicines, it must be with due correctives, and you must take great care of yourselves, lest that turn to your prejudice, and become a snare and a trap, which was intended for your health and welfare.

Allow yourselves in mirth, as far as will consist with sober-mindedness, and no further; be merry and wise; never let your mirth transgress the laws of piety, charity, or modesty, nor intrench upon your time for devotion and the service of God. Wise men will always reckon him over fond of his mirth, that will rather lose his friend than his jest; much more may he be reckoned so, that will rather lose his God and a good conscience.

Never make sport with the scripture and sacred things, but let that which is serious always be spoken of with seriousness, for it is ill jesting with edge-tools. Take heed lest your mirth exceed due bounds, and transport you into any indecencies: that you

31

give not yourselves too great a liberty, and then think to excuse it by saying, 'Am not I in sport?' (*Prov. 26, v.19*). Set a double guard at such a time before the door of your lips, lest you offend with your tongues; and especially keep your hearts with all diligence.

Let the inward thought still be serious; and in the midst of your greatest mirth, retain a disposition habitually serious, and a reigning affection to spiritual and divine things, such as will make you indifferent to all vain mirth and pleasure, and set you above it, and enable you to look upon that with a holy contempt, which so many spend so much of their time in with so great a complacency.

A serious Christian, though to relax himself, and entertain his friends, he may allow himself a little mirth and recreation, yet he will make it to appear he is not in that as in his element, but he knows better pleasures, and has given them the preference. A believing foretaste of the milk and honey of Canaan, is enough to put the mouth quite out of taste to the garlic and onions of Egypt.

But while I am pressing you that are young to be always serious, habitually so, always well-affected to serious work, what shall we think of those that are never serious — that are always on the merry pin — always jesting, always bantering, so that you never know when they speak in earnest — that are always in pursuit of some sensual pleasure or other, and never know what it is to be one quarter of an hour serious, from the beginning of the year to the end of it? Certainly they forget, that 'for all these things, God shall bring them into judgment,' and they know not how soon.

O that this laughter might be turned into the mourning of true penitents, and this joy into the heaviness of sincere converts; that it may not be turned, as otherwise it certainly will be, into the weeping and wailing of damned sinners! The same Jesus that said, 'Blessed are they that mourn, for they shall be comforted,' hath said also, 'Wo unto you that laugh now, for you shall mourn and weep' (*Luke 6, v.25*).

Shall I now prevail with you that are young to value wisdom

above wit, and that which helps to make you serious above that which helps to make you merry; and to take as much pleasure in gravity as others do in vanity? It will be the honour of your youth — will arm you against the temptations you are surrounded with — and will not only mark you for something considerable in this world, but for something infinitely more so in the other world.

And if you understand yourselves right, I dare say, one hour spent in the employments and enjoyments of a sober, serious mind, will afford you more true comfort in the reflection, than many spent in mirth and gaiety, because it will certainly pass so much better in the account another day.

If you take the world for your guide, you will be bid to laugh and be fat — will be told, that an ounce of mirth is worth a pound of sorrow; but if you will attend to the dictates of the word of God (and it is fit the word that must judge us hereafter, should rule us now), that will tell you, that 'sorrow is better than laughter;' and that it is 'better to go to the house of mourning, than to the house of feasting; for by the sadness of the countenance the heart is made better,' it is made serious.

And thus you see what it is to be sober-minded, and how much of your duty it takes in; but are you content it should take in all this? Can you say, that though in many things you come short, yet you esteem all these precepts, and all the things contained in them, to be right, and therefore 'hate every false way'? You will then be very willing to have this sober-mindedness further pressed upon you.

PART TWO

Why Be Sober-minded?

Let us now see what considerations are proper, and may be powerful to make young people in all these respects sober-minded. And will you that are young, apply your minds a little to these things?

onsider how noble and excellent that rank of
beings is that you are of — how far advanced above that of the
beasts — and, consequently, how unjust you are both to God
and to yourselves, if by incogitancy, inconsideration, or the
indulgence of any brutish appetite or passion, you level
yourselves with the beasts that perish. What have you your
reason for, if you do not make use of it? Your mind, if you do not
take care to keep yourselves of a sound mind? Or, if you mind
not that for the sake of which you had your minds given you?
'Show yourselves men, bring it again to mind, O ye transgressors' (*Isa. 46, v.8*).

Sinners would become saints, if they would but show themselves men; for the service of Christ is a reasonable service, and
those that are wicked are unreasonable men; be persuaded
therefore to act rationally, and to save the nobler powers of
reason from being tied up and overpowered by this and the other
rebellious lust and passion.

You brought rational souls with you into the world; but think
how long the seeds of reason lay buried under the clods before
they began to spring up; how long those sparks of a divine fire
seemed lost in the embers during the years of infancy, when you
were not capable of the consideration we are persuading you to;
yet then God took care of you, provided for you, and did you
good, when you were not able to do him any service; study
therefore, now you are come to the use of reason, what honours,
and what dignities shall be done to him, who was then careful for
you with all that care. Study how you shall redeem the time that
was then unavoidably lost, by making so much the more use of
your reason now.

Think, likewise, how much time runs waste in sleep — how
many hours pass every day, during which the operations of
reason are suspended, and fancy is all that while busy at work in
a thousand foolish dreams — yet then God preserves us, and
gives his angels a charge over us.

Let us, therefore, when we are awake, set reason on work,

6

find it employment, and support its authority by sober-mindedness; and let not the conversation of the day be as idle and impertinent as the dreams of the night are, as I fear with many it is, both young and old.

Think, likewise, how piteous the case of those is that are deprived of the use of their reason — that were born idiots, or are fallen into deep melancholy, or into distraction and frenzy — that are incapable of thinking, speaking, and acting rationally, and are put out of the possession, government, and enjoyment of themselves; this might have been your case; it is God's great mercy to you that it is not so: nor can you be secure, but that some time or other it may be so.

You would dread it as the greatest affliction, not be able to use your reason — and will you not dread as a great sin, not to use it well, and as it should be used, now you are able?

When St Paul would prove to the most noble Festus, that he was not beside himself, that he was not mad: his plea is, 'I speak the words of truth and soberness;' as if those that do not speak the words of truth and soberness, all whose talk is banter and vanity, were no better than mad, and beside themselves. O that such young people as are thus taken in the snare of carnal mirth, and are in effect made delirious by it, as you may perceive by the rambles of their talk, would at length recover their senses, return to their wits, and be sober-minded! that they would, like the prodigal son, come to themselves, and come to a resolution to stay no longer in the devil's fields, to feed the swine of their own sinful lusts; but to return to their Father's house, where they will be happy, and shall be welcome!

When Christ was here upon earth, healing all manner of sickness, and all manner of disease, there was no one sort of patients that he had greater numbers of than such as were lunatic, and their lunacy was the effect of their being possessed with the devil. It was the miserable case of many young people. We find parents making complaints of this kind concerning their children; one has a daughter, another has a son, grievously vexed with a devil; but Christ healed them all, dispossessed Satan, and so restored them to the possession of their own souls;

and it is said of some whom he thus relieved, that they then sat 'at the feet of Jesus clothed and in their right mind;' it is the word used in the text (*Luke 8, v.35*).

As far as sin reigns in you, Satan reigns; and your souls are in his possession. Christ, by casting out devils, gave a specimen and indication of the great design of his gospel and grace, which was to cure men of their spiritual frenzy, by breaking the power of Satan in them. O that you would therefore apply yourselves to him — submit to the word of his grace — pray for the Spirit of his grace. And by this it will appear, that both these have had their due influence upon you, if you sit at the feet of Jesus in your right mind — in a sober mind. And indeed you never come to your right mind, till you do sit down at the feet of Jesus, to learn of him, and be ruled by him; you never are truly rational creatures, till in Christ you become new creatures.

2. All are Sinners

You are all sinners, and guilty before God; conceived in iniquity, born in sin, you are by nature children of disobedience, and children of wrath; whether you have ever thought of it or not, certainly it is so; the scripture hath concluded you all under sin, and consequently under a sentence of death, like that of a physician upon his patient, when he pronounceth his disease mortal; nay, like that of a judge upon the prisoner, when he pronounceth his crime capital, so that both ways your danger is imminent and extreme. And shall not the consideration of this prevail to make you sober?

Were your bodies under some threatening disease, which, in all probability, would in a little time cut off the thread of your life, I believe that would make you serious — that would make you solemn; were you condemned to die shortly by the hand of justice, that would sober you; and is not the death and ruin of an immortal soul more to be dreaded than that of a mortal body? And should not the danger of that give a louder alarm to the most secure, and cast a greater damp upon the most jovial, than of the other?

And when you are told, that though the disease is mortal, it is

not incurable; though the crime is capital, it is not unpardonable; how should that yet further prevail to make you serious —
to make you very solicitous, very industrious to get the disease
healed, and the crime forgiven? Your case will not allow any of
your time or thoughts to run waste, or to be trifled away, but you
have need by sober-mindedness to employ both in a due attendance to the things that belong to your everlasting peace.

You are sinners, and therefore have reason to think very
meanly and humbly of yourselves, not to expect applauses, or
resent contempts, nor to aim at great things in the world. What
have such vile wretches as we are to be proud of, or to promise
ourselves in this world, who owe our lives, which we have a
thousand times forfeited, to the divine patience?

You are sinners, and if yet you are in a state of sin, 'in the gall
of bitterness and bond of iniquity,' the misery of your state is
enough to give an effectual check to your vain mirth, and would
do it, if you knew and considered it. 'Rejoice not, O Israel, for
joy, as other people, for thou hast gone a-whoring from thy God'
(*Hos. 9, v.1*). Joy is forbidden fruit to wicked people. There
cannot be a more monstrous absurdity, than that which they
are guilty of, 'who say to the Almighty, Depart from us;' who set
him at a distance, set him at defiance, and yet 'take the timbrel
and harp, and rejoice at the sound of the organ, they spend their
days in wealth' (*Job 21, vv.12,13*).

If through grace the power of sin is broken in you, and you are
delivered from the wrath to come, and being in Christ, there is
no condemnation to you, yet the very remembrance of the
misery and danger you were in, and are delivered from — how
near you were to the pit's brink, and how you were snatched as
brands out of the burning — should make you serious. You still
carry a body of death about with you, which should make you
cry out, O wretched creatures that we are! We are compassed
about with enemies that war against your souls; you have not yet
put off the harness, but have reason still to 'fear, lest a promise
being left you of entering into rest, any of you should seem to
come short;' and this is enough to make you considerate, and
cautious, and sober-minded.

In short, till you have by faith in Christ made your peace with God, and are become sincere Christians, you have no reason to rejoice at all; and when you have done it, and have some comfortable evidence of a blessed change through grace wrought in you, you will then have better things to rejoice in than this world can furnish you with; and having tasted spiritual pleasures, will be dead to all the delights of sense; offer them to those that know no better.

3. Setting Out

You are setting out in a world of sorrows and snares, of troubles and temptations, and therefore are concerned to be sober-minded, that you may be armed accordingly, so as that the troubles of the world may not rob you of your peace, nor the temptations of it rob you of your purity. Your way lies through a wilderness, 'a land of darkness and drought,' and nothing but sober-mindedness will carry you safe through it to Canaan.

Now you are young, and have the world before you, you are apt to flatter yourselves with a conceit that every thing will be safe and pleasant. Your mountain, you think, stands so strong, that it cannot be moved; that nothing can shake either your integrity, or your prosperity; but you little know what this world is, and what snares there are in every condition of life, and every company, in all employments, and in all enjoyments.

And if you be careless and vain, and live at large, you make yourselves an easy prey to the tempter, and are in danger of being carried away by the course of this world; you have need therefore to take heed of yourselves, and to keep your souls diligently, that is, to be sober-minded; for considering the corruption that is in the world through lust, and the corruption that is in your own hearts, what may we not fear when they come together?

When the restraints of education are taken off, and you begin to find yourselves at liberty, you will meet with so many enticing sins and sinners, that you will be in danger of falling in licentiousness, and being undone, unless the impressions of your education still abide, unless by this sober-mindedness you still be your own parents, your own masters, your own tutors, and by an established virtue, through the grace of God, a law to yourselves.

You know not what trials and troubles you may be reserved for, but you know that man, who is born of a woman, is but of few days, and full of trouble — his crosses certain, more or less — a cross to be taken up daily, his comforts uncertain: and should not this make you sober? that when afflictions come, they may not be so terrible as they are to those, who, by indulging themselves in mirth and pleasure, have made themselves like the tender and delicate woman, that would not set so much as the sole of her foot to the ground, for tenderness and delicacy (*Deut. 28, v.56*). Even the common calamities of human life press hard upon such, and wound deep; whereas, those that live a sober, serious, self-denying life, are, like Christ, 'acquainted with grief,' have made it familiar to them, and can the easier reconcile themselves to it.

Some of you, perhaps, are sickly, and often out of health; you carry ailments about you, which tell you what you are, and you are inexcusable if you be not thereby made sober, if that does not deaden you to the delights of sense, and lower your expectations from the creature, and dispose you to serious work. By the sickness of the body the heart should be made better; many a one's has been, the uncertainty of whose bodily health has conduced very much to the health of their souls. Those do indeed walk contrary to God, that allow themselves in vanity, while they carry about with them sensible tokens of their mortality.

But even the most strong and healthy may die in their full strength, and must die at last. We are all dying daily; death is working in us, and we are walking towards it, and shall not that make us sober? Theirs was an unpardonable crime that said, 'Let us eat and drink, for to-morrow we die' (*Isa. 22, vv.13,14*), that when they were minded by the prophet of the near approach of death, as a reason why they should repent and reform speedily, turned it a quite contrary way, and argued, If we must have a short life, let it be a merry one. 'Surely,' saith God, 'this iniquity shall not be purged from you.'

'The end of all things is at hand,' is near at hand with us, 'be ye therefore sober;' that whenever our Lord shall come, we may be in a good frame to meet him. When we consider what our bodies will be shortly, how near a-kin they are to corruption and the worms, we shall see little reason to pamper them, and to bring them up delicately, for we are hastening to the house of darkness, where the voice of mirth is no more heard.

4. Others are ruined

You see many young people about you ruined and undone, and it was for want of being sober-minded. Many, perhaps, you have known, or might have observed, that were born of good parents, had a religious education, set out well, were for some time hopeful, and promised fair with buds and blossoms, but ended in the flesh, after they had begun in the Spirit, and it was for want of consideration; they could not be persuaded to think soberly; they were 'drawn away of their own lust and enticed;' and those enticements were hearkened to when a deaf ear was turned to Wisdom's calls, and to all the dictates of reason and conscience, they would not hearken to the voice of those charmers, charming never so wisely.

Some have out-run their apprenticeships — others have foolishly thrown themselves away in marriage — others have set up and made a flourish a while, but have soon broke, and become bankrupts, either by living high, or by grasping at more business than they could grasp; some have been carried away by atheistical and profane notions, and others by a loose and vain conversation; all of which would have been happily prevented, if they had been humble and discreet, and duly governed their appetites and passions.

Others' harms should be your warnings, to take heed of the rocks they split upon. Sir Richard Blackmore, in his heroic poem of Job, thus gives the reason of Job's pious care concerning his sons, after the days of their feasting were gone about:

For he with mournful eyes had often spy'd,
Scatter'd on pleasure's smooth, but treacherous tide,
The spoils of virtue overpower'd by sense,
And floating wrecks of ruin'd innocence.

5. On Trial

You are here in this world upon your trial for heaven. O that you would firmly believe this, not only that you are hastening apace into eternity, but that it will certainly be to you a comfortable, or a miserable eternity, according to what you are and do, while you are in the body! And this consideration, one would think, should make you sober.

Eternal life is set before you, eternal happiness is in vision and fruition of God; you may make it sure, if it be not your own fault; may lay hold on it, if you look about you now. There are substantial honours, satisfying pleasures, and true riches, in comparison with which all the riches, honours, and pleasures of this world are empty names and shadows: these may be your portion for ever — they shall be so, if by a patient continuance in well-doing, through Christ, you seek for this glory, honour, and immortality. You are here probationers for the best preferment, for a place in the new Jerusalem; you stand candidates for a crown, a kingdom, incorruptible, undefiled, and that fadeth not away; you stand fair for it.

Is it not time to think then? — to think seriously — and soberly to apply yourselves to that business for which you were sent into this world, and which, if it be done faithfully, you may remove with comfort to another world; but if not, your remove to that world will be terrible! You ought to be serious and circumspect now, because as you spend your time, so you are likely to spend your eternity; and a great deal of work you have to do, and but little time to do it in.

Let me put the case to you, as to this world: If a wise and wealthy man should take one of you, that had but little, and tell you, you should come into his family, and he would provide food and clothing for you for one year, and if you carried yourself well for that year, would submit to the prudent discipline of his family, would be observant of him, and take care to please him, that then at the year's end he would give you ten thousand pounds; but if you were rude and ungovernable, he would turn you out of doors; would not this put you upon considering? Would it not make you sober? Would you not deny yourselves the gratification of many a desire, for fear of displeasing such a benefactor? If he were never so humoursome you would humour him, when it were so much your interest.

This is your case; the time of your probation is but short; the terms are easy and reasonable; the God you are to please is not hard to be pleased, nor will impose any thing upon you but what becomes you, and will be pleasant to you. The happiness he proposes is infinitely more worth than thousands of gold and silver, and the security he gives, is the inviolable promise of one that cannot lie nor deceive; the misery, if you come short of it, is worse than being turned out of doors — it is to be cast into utter darkness.

Life and death — good and evil — the blessing and the curse — are set before you, and will you not then set your hearts to all the words which we testify unto you? Will you not think soberly, that you may make sure work in a matter of such vast importance, on which your lives, and the lives of your souls depend? You are here upon your good behaviour, and therefore are concerned to behave yourselves well; for if you do not, 'Son, remember,' will be a dreadful peal rung in your ears shortly; remember how fair you stood for happiness, and what the morsel of meat was, for which, like profane Esau, you sold that birth-right.

6. Future Judgment

You must shortly go to judgment. With the consideration of this, Solomon endeavours to make his young man sober, who is for walking in the way of his heart, and in the sight of his eyes; 'Know thou, that for all these things, God will bring thee into judgment.' And thou that makest a jest of every thing, shalt not be able to turn that off with a jest hereafter, however thou mayest think to do it now (*Eccl. 11, v.9*). This likewise he urgeth upon his pupil in the close of that book, as a reason why he should be religious: 'By these, my son, be admonished to fear God and keep his commandments, for God shall bring every work into judgment, with every secret thing' (*Eccl. 12, vv.12,13,14*).

Young men that have strict masters, who will call them to an account how they spend their time, and how they go on with their business, are thereby obliged to industry and care; whereas, if the master be careless, the servant is in temptation to be so too; but know that you have a Master in heaven, whose eye is always upon you, and follows you closer than the eye of any master on earth can; he knows and observes all you do, all you say, all you think, and an account is kept of it in the book of his omniscience, and your own conscience. These books will shortly be opened, and not only all reviewed, but you will be judged accordingly; and are you not then concerned to think, and speak, and act accordingly?

When you are vain and profane, should not this be a check upon you, and make you sober to think — How will this look when it comes to be looked over again? How will it pass, when I pass my trials for eternity?

Your bodies are mortal, your souls are immortal, therefore let not sin reign either in the one or in the other; you are dying, are dying daily; in the midst of life, nay, in the beginning of it, we are in death; you may die this day, may die in youth, and the number of your months be cut off in the midst; and you know, that after death the judgment; and as your state is fixed in the particular judgment at death, so it will be found in the general judgment at the end of time, and so it will remain to eternity. How awful, how dreadful the appearance of the Judge will be in the great day, the word of God has again and again told us.

Knowing therefore those terrors of the Lord, the terrors of that day, we implore men — we beseech young men — to be sober-minded, and therefore to let their moderation, that is, their sober-mindedness, their good government and management of themselves, be known unto all men, because the Lord is at hand. 'The Judge standeth before the door.'

45

PART THREE

What is Needed?

You see now what is expected from you that are young, and how justly it is expected, you see both from the word of God; and now, shall I entreat you to make use of what I have said, to make it useful to yourselves, that this discourse may not be lost upon you?

    1. Self-examination

    2. Exhortation

1. Self-examination

I want you to examine yourselves, and take heed of being mistaken in your judgment concerning yourselves. Can your hearts witness for you, that through the grace of God, by remembering yourselves and your Creator in the days of your youth, you are become in some measure sober-minded, and answer this beautiful character of young people?

I hope I speak to many such, and the misery is, that those who most need these instructions and warnings, come least in the way of them; they will not hear them, will not read them, because they resolve they will not heed them, or be ruled by them. But to you that are sober-minded, I say, as Christ did to the faithful ones in Thyatira, 'I will lay upon you no other burden, but that which you have already;' and I am sure you will agree to call it a light burden: hold fast till Christ comes; hold fast your integrity; hold fast your sober-mindedness.

Some are more inclined to soberness in their natural temper than others are, to them these laws of sober-mindedness will be easier than to others; but to them that are not so, though it be more difficult, yet withal it is more necessary. Wisdom, and grace, and consideration, are intended for the checking of disorders of the natural temper. But take heed lest you deceive yourselves, and be more forward than there is cause to rank yourselves among the sober-minded, and to think that you need not these admonitions.

It is not a sober look that will serve, though that is graceful enough, if it be not affected and forced; but it is the sober mind that we are pressing earnestly upon you; examine that now, for God will examine that, and judge of you by it, when you shall find that 'to be carnally minded is death, but to be spiritually minded is life and peace.'

2. Exhortation

I want you to exhort yourselves. So some read that which we translate, 'exhort one another;' preach to your own hearts, preach over this message to them. Let all young people charge, and admonish, and encourage themselves to be sober-minded.

Let those that have loose notions in religion, and are fond of any suggestions, though never so absurd, which derogate from the authority and honour of the scriptures and revealed religion, exhort themselves to be sober-minded and not to be carried about with every wind, nor carried away from the great principles of Christianity, by the craft of them who lie in wait to deceive, and bring them to downright atheism.

Let those that are drawn in, or are in danger of being drawn into the ruining sins of drunkenness or uncleanness, that have been so fatal to multitudes of young people, exhort themselves to be sober-minded, to sit down and consider seriously what will be in the end thereof, and how dreadful that destruction is which these vicious courses certainly lead to. Except you repent and reform, you must perish — must eternally perish — if the word of God be true, you must; and how miserable will your case be if you bring it to this dilemma, that either God must be false, or you must be damned?

Let those that spend their time in carnal mirth, and sensual pleasures, whose business is nothing but sport and pastime, and their converse nothing but banter and buffoonery, exhort themselves to be sober-minded, sometimes to be serious, and consider themselves; and try if they can make it as pleasant to themselves to think in earnest, as it is now to walk in jest: for I am sure, it will be abundantly more profitable.

Let those young people that are addicted to gambling, and flatter themselves with hopes of getting that easily and quickly, which they love above any thing, but are not willing to be at the pains of getting honestly, exhort themselves to be sober-minded; and to consider what a sinful way this is of trading with what they have, and which they cannot in faith pray to God to bless and prosper them in: to consider that whether they win or lose, they can have no true comfort, no joy of their gains, for it is wealth gotten by vanity, that has a curse attending it, nor any support under their losses, for they are owing to their own sin and folly.

How many apprentices have been brought by their love of gambling to rob their masters, and so to ruin themselves! And how many young gentlemen have sunk their estates, and young tradesmen their stocks and business by it; and will you for want of one sober thought, split upon the same rock? Let those who are allured into this snare — into the beginning of it — dread it, and keep at the utmost distance from it; and let those who are taken in it, break out of it immediately, with resolution: 'Do this now, my son, deliver thyself as a roe from the hand of the hunter.'

Let young dealers in the world, that are entering into business, exhort themselves to be sober-minded — to set out under the conduct of religion and true wisdom — to love their business, to apply themselves, and accommodate themselves to it. Let them learn betimes to take care, for nothing will be done to purpose without it — to attend the work of their callings with diligence, and order the affairs of them with discretion — and in all their ways to acknowledge God; then are they likely to prosper, and to have good success.

Let young professors of religion, that by the grace of God have escaped the corruption that is in the world, and given up their names to Jesus Christ, exhort themselves to be sober-minded in their profession. Let them take heed of conceitedness, and spiritual pride, of confidence in themselves, and their own judgment and ability; let them aim to be best, rather than to be greatest in the kingdom of God among men. Let them take heed of running into extremes, and of falling into bigotry and censoriousness; let them be sober in their opinions of truth and falsehood, good and evil, of others and of themselves; expecting that age and experience will rectify many of their present mistakes.

Let young scholars, whose genius leads them to books and learning, exhort themselves to be sober-minded; you soon find that you must be serious, must be much so, must learn to think, and to think closely, or you will never make anything of it. It is not enough to read, but you must study and digest what you read. But that is not all; in your pursuits of knowledge you must be sober, not exercising yourselves in things too high for you, nor boasting yourselves of your attainments.

Be humble in the use of what you do know, using it for edification, not for ostentation; it is but a windy knowledge that puffs up; that only is good for something that does good (*1 Cor. 8, v.1*). Be humble likewise in your inquiries after what you would know; not coveting to be wise above what is written, or to intrude into those things which you have not seen, as many who are vainly puffed up with a fleshly mind, but be wise unto sobriety. Be willing to be in the dark about which God has not thought fit to reveal, and in doubt about that which he has not thought fit to determine.

PART FOUR

The Benefits of a Sober Mind

To recommend this sober-mindedness to all of you that are young, this seriousness, and sedateness of spirit, and aptness to consider; will you be convinced of what great advantage it will be to you every way?

1. An Escape

You will escape the vanity that childhood and youth is subject to, and rescue those precious years from it. It will keep them from running waste, as commonly they do, like water spilt upon the ground, which cannot be gathered up again, and will do much towards the filling up of the empty spaces, even of those years. When Solomon had observed, that childhood and youth is vanity, he immediately adds for the cure of that vanity, 'Remember now thy Creator in the days of thy youth,' that is, in one word, be serious.

By using yourselves to consideration, you will come to be aware of the snares your spiritual enemies lay for you, of the snake under the green grass, and will not be imposed upon so easily as many are by the wiles of Satan; and by habituating yourselves to self-denial and mortification of the flesh, and a holy contempt of this world, you will wrest the most dangerous weapons out of the hand of the strong man armed, and will take from him that part of his armour in which he most trusted, for it is by the world and the flesh that he mostly fights against us; nay, and this sober-mindedness will put upon you the whole armour of God, that you may be able to stand in the evil day, and so to resist the devil, as that he may flee from you.

This sober-mindedness will prevent many a temptation which a vain mind invites, and courts, and throws men into the way of; and will shut and lock the door against the tempter, who, when he finds it so, will give it up; and his agents will be apt to do so too, concluding it in vain to tempt the sober mind; they will do as Naomi, who, when she saw that Ruth was steadfastly minded, left off speaking to her.

2. In Favour with God

You will recommend yourselves to the favour of God, and of all wise and good men — you will obtain that good name which is better than precious ointment, and more fragrant — a name for good things with God and good people. God will love those that love him, and seek him early; and will never forget this kindness of your youth for serious godliness.

If you thus give him the first of your first-fruits, it will be an acceptable offering to him. The beloved disciple was the youngest. And it is said of that young man, who asked that serious question, and asked it soberly, 'Good master, what shall I do to inherit eternal life?' that 'Jesus, beholding him, loved him,' (*Mark 10, vv.17,21*). As he was likewise well pleased with another, who answered discreetly, like one that had a sober mind (*Mat. 12, v.34*).

And that humility and quietness of spirit, which is one branch of this sober mind, is an ornament, which wherever it is found, especially in young people, is in the sight of God of great price; and that is valuable indeed which he values, and by it we ought to value ourselves.

Nor is it an argument to be despised by you, that all sober people that know you, will love you, and will have no greater joy than to see you live soberly; but it is an argument the rather to be insisted upon by us, because young people are commonly very much influenced by reputation, and have an eye to that more than anything in the government of themselves, and the choice of their way.

Now it is certain, reputation is on religion's side, and if the matter be rightly understood, will help to turn the scale for sober-mindedness. It is true, there are some — there are many, to whom a young man will recommend himself by being loose and extravagant, and talking at random against that which is serious; but what kind of people are they? Are they not the fools in Israel? Are they not drunks or fools, whose valuation of persons and things is not at all to be valued?

But do not all discreet and considerate people esteem a young man that is sober, and show him respect, and converse with him, and put a confidence in him. It is the character of a citizen of Zion, that in his eyes a vile person is condemned; though he set up for a wit or a beau, yet if he be loose and profane, he despiseth him as a fool, and a flash; but he honours them that fear the Lord, and live conscientiously.

Now, to which of these would you recommend yourselves? Whose opinion would you covet to stand right in, to stand high in? Would you not choose to have credit with men of virtue and probity, and that are themselves in reputation for wisdom and honour, and to be laid in their bosoms, rather than to be hugged, and caressed, and cried up by those that, being slaves to their pleasures, can never be masters of true reason?

Especially considering, that those young people who are truly sober, serious, and conscientious, provided they take care to avoid affectation, and superciliousness, will be loved and respected even by those that are themselves loose and vain; and will be manifested in their consciences one time or other, that they are the most valuable young men. And I think it is worth considering, and would bear a debate, whether ordinarily sober serious people do not love their friends and companions better, than vain loose people do theirs, and are not more ready to do them true service?

3. A Useful Life

You will prepare for a useful life, if it please God you live long, and for a comfortable one. Those that are sober-minded when they are young, as they are thereby fortified against every evil word and work, so they are furnished for every good word and work, and are likely to be in their day vessels of honour fit for our Master's use, while the ludicrous and unthinking, live to be at the best the unprofitable burdens of the earth, and good for nothing.

Young people that are sober, are likely to be good, and do good in every relation and condition of life — that are sober when they are children and servants — that do the duties, and improve the advantages of their learning age, and behave themselves prudently then — are in the fitting up hereafter to have the charge of families themselves, to which they are likely to be great blessings, and to the places in which they live.

They will not only be the joy of their parents' hearts while they live, but an honour to their memories when they are gone; and thus the children will rise up and call the discreet and virtuous mother blessed, by treading in her steps, and producing the good fruits of their prudent and religious education.

Young men that are sober-minded are likely to be in time serviceable to the communities they are members of, civil or sacred, in a higher or lower sphere. They may be called to the magistracy or ministry — to serve the state, to serve the church; but few ever come to do real service or credit to either, or to be of account in either of those posts of honour, unless they be sober-minded when they are young. Lose the morning, and you lose the day.

But though they may not arrive to such a public station, yet they may in a private capacity be eminently useful to their neighbours, in the things of the world, and to their fellow-christians in divine things, and so be instruments of glory to God. They that are sober-minded when they are young, if they go on as they begin, what will the wisdom be which the multitude of their years will teach? Obadiah that feared the Lord from his youth, came to fear him greatly. Young saints, we hope, will be eminent ones.

4. A Happy Death

You will prepare for a happy death, if it please God you should die quickly, and may then die cheerfully. O that young people were so wise as to consider their latter end not only as sure, but as near! It is folly for the youngest, and strongest, and most healthy, to put far from them the day of death, when death is every day working in us.

Now, the best preparation you can make for it, if you should die in youth, is to live soberly. Then the sting of it will be taken out, through Christ, and consequently the terror of it taken off; and therefore though you may pray with the psalmist, 'O my God, take me not away in the midst of my days,' yet if the cup may not pass away, you need not dread it, you know the worst that death can do you, if it shorten your life on earth, that will be abundantly made up in a better life.

Abijah, that sober youth, in whom was found some good thing towards the Lord God of Israel in the house of Jeroboam, dies in the flower of his age, but there is no harm done him, he comes to his grave in peace, and goes to heaven triumphantly (*1 Kings 14, v.13*).

Whereas, those that are loose and extravagant, if they die in youth (as Elihu speaks, Job 36, v.14) 'their soul dieth' — so it is in the original — they are spiritually dead, twice dead; while they lived in pleasure, they were dead though they lived; and therefore when they die in sin, they are twice dead, and their life, their life on the other side death, is among the unclean, among the Sodomites — so the margin reads it — who suffer the vengeance of eternal fire, Jude 7.

PART FIVE

How to become Sober-minded

Let me now close with five general directions to young people, which may be of use to them, in order to the making of them sober-minded.

1. Adopt Sober Principles
2. Food for Thought — The Law and the Gospel
3. Choose Your Company
4. Choose Your Reading
5. Be Diligent

1. Adopt Sober Principles

Espouse sober principles; for men are, as their principles are. In these avoid extremes; and in the less weighty matters of the law, keep the mean, that you may reserve your zeal for the great things of God, the things that belong to your everlasting peace. Take heed on the one hand of bigotry in the circumstantials of religion, and on the other hand of lukewarmness and indifferency in the essentials of it.

Fix such principles as these to yourselves with reference to the main matter — that God's favour is better than life, and his displeasure worse than death; that sin is the greatest evil; that the soul is the man, and that is best for us that is best for our souls: that Jesus Christ is all in all to us, and we are undone without an interest in him; that it is as much our wisdom, as it is our duty, to be religious; that the world has not that in it, which will make us happy; that time, and the things of time, are nothing in comparison with eternity, and the things of eternity.

These, and such as these, are principles of eternal truth, and our firm belief of them, and adherence to them, will be to us of eternal consequence. And as to other things, let your principle be, that 'God is no respecter of persons, but in every nation, he that fears God, and works righteousness, is accepted of him;' and therefore ought to be so of us: 'that the kingdom of God is not meat and drink, but righteousness and peace, and joy in the Holy Ghost; and he that in these things serveth Christ, is acceptable to God, and approved of men.'

By such principles as these, keep up moderation and sobermindedness in your profession of religion, which will contribute much to the promoting of it in every thing else.

2. Food for Thought — The Law and the Gospel

Dwell much upon such considerations as are proper to make you soberminded. Be frequent in meditation upon serious things — the great things of the law and gospel — and let not them be looked upon as foreign things. As you think in your hearts, so you are. If the imagination of the thought of the heart be vain and corrupt, if that eye be evil, the whole man will be accordingly; but if that be serious, the affections and aims will be sober too.

However you may allow the natural thoughts to be sometimes diverting, the inward thoughts must be reserved for that which is directing. Think much of the eye of God which is always upon you, that you may be careful to approve yourselves to him in every thing; of the glory of God which you ought always to have your eye upon, that you may answer the end of your creation. Think much of the many sins you have committed against God, that you may give diligence to make sure the pardon of them; and of the many mercies you have received from God, that you may study what returns you shall make for his favour. Think much of the opportunities you enjoy, that you may be busy to improve them; and of the spiritual enemies you are encompassed about with, that you may be sober and vigilant in guarding against them.

The four last things, death and judgment, heaven and hell, are commonly recommended as proper subjects of meditation, in order to the making of the mind serious. Because the end of all things is at hand, and that end an entrance upon a state without end, be you therefore sober, and check vanity with that consideration.

I have somewhere read of one, that had been a great courtier and statesman in Queen Elizabeth's time — I think it was secretary Walsingham — that in his advanced years he retired into privacy in the country, where some of his pleasant companions came to see him, and told him he was melancholy: 'No,' saith he, 'I am serious, and it is fit I should be so, for all are serious round about me, and why then should not you and I be serious?'

God is serious in observing of us — Christ is serious in interceding for us — the Spirit is serious in striving with us — the truths of God are serious truths — his laws, his promises, his threatenings, all serious — angels are serious in their administrations to us — our spiritual enemies serious in their attempts against us — glorified saints are serious in the embraces of divine love — poor damned sinners cannot but be serious under the pourings out of divine wrath, and we ourselves shall be serious shortly.

3. Choose Your Company

Choose sober company. Nothing is of greater consequence to young people, than what company they keep, for we insensibly grow like those with whom we converse, especially with whom we delight to converse. Many that were thought to be very soberly inclined, have had their good inclinations turned the contrary way, by keeping vain and loose company, which perhaps at first they were not aware of any danger by, but thought their conversation innocent enough. Though ill company perhaps bears more blame sometimes than it deserves, from those who think to excuse themselves by laying the fault on their companions, yet it is agreed to have been of most pernicious consequence to multitudes that set out well.

If therefore you would be wise and good, choose such for your associates and bosom-friends as will give you good advice, and set you good examples; he that walketh with wise men, is wise, or would be wise, and he shall be wise, when a companion of fools is deceived, and shall be destroyed. Keep at a distance from loose and vain company, for who can touch pitch and not be defiled? who can converse familiarly with those that are wicked and profane, and not contract guilt, or grief, or both?

If you resolve, as David did, to keep the commandments of your God, you must say to evil-doers as he did, 'Depart from me,' (*Ps. 119, v.115*) and be as he was, companions of all those that fear God, ver. 63. and let your delight be in the excellent ones of the earth, the sober ones.

4. Choose Your Reading

Read sober books. Those that are given to reading, are as much under the influence of the books they read, as of the persons they converse with, and therefore in the choice of them you need to be very cautious, and take advice. Nothing more prompts vanity, especially among the refined part of mankind, than romances and plays, and loose poems; and thus even their solitudes and retirements, which we hope might contribute to their seriousness, are lost, and make them more vain, and more ingeniously so.

Let us therefore take the same method to make us sober, more sober; converse with those books which are substantial and judicious, out of which we may learn wisdom. The Book of God is given us on purpose to make us wise to salvation, make it familiar to you, and let it dwell in you richly. Let it lead you, let it talk with you; and do you follow it, and talk with it, (*Prov. 6, v.22*). And many other good books we have to help us to understand and apply the scripture, which we should be conversant with. Inquire not for merry books, songs, and jests, but serious books, which will help to put you into, and keep you in a serious frame.

5. Be Diligent

Abound much in sober work. Habits are contracted by frequent acts; if therefore you would have a sober mind, employ yourselves much in meditation and prayer, and other devout and holy exercises. And in these let your hearts be fixed, and let all that is within you be employed. Be much in secret worship, as well as diligent and constant in your attendance on public ordinances; those who neglect these cannot but lose their seriousness.

And see to it that you be very serious when you are about serious work, that you profane not the holy things. I look upon it to be in young people as happy an indication of a serious mind, and as hopeful an omen of a serious life, as any other, to be reverent and serious in the worship of God. For it is a sign the vanity of the mind runs high and strong indeed, when even there it will not be restrained from indecencies; and he is loose indeed that is 'almost in all evil in the midst of the congregation and assembly,' (*Prov. 5, v.14*).

The greatness of the God with whom you have to do, and the greatness of the concern you have to do with him in, when you are engaged in his worship, should strike an awe upon you, and make you serious.

And have this in your eye in all religious exercises, that by them you may be made more serious; and that the impressions of other holy exercises may be the deeper, and take the faster hold, let me advise young people that are sober-minded, to come betimes to the ordinance of the Lord's supper.

Let me press it upon them, not only as a duty they owe to Christ, but as that which will be of great advantage to themselves to strengthen their resolutions, with purpose of heart to cleave to the Lord. Those who keep off from it, it is either because they know they are not sober-minded, or because they are not determined to continue so; but none of you will own either of those reasons. Delay not therefore by that most sacred solemn bond, to join yourselves to the Lord in a perpetual covenant, never to be forgotten.

And how do you like this sober, serious work you have now been about in reading this discourse? Have you been in it as your element — or as a fish upon dry ground? Have you suffered this word of exhortation, and bidden it welcome? Shall I leave you all resolved in the strength of God's grace, that now in the days of your youth you will be sober-minded? If so, the Lord keep it always in the imagination of the thought of your heart, and by writing the law of sobriety there, establish your way before him!